...Or Something: Words I Can't Say Out Loud

Alexia Miron

BookLeaf Publishing

Presentation by *BookLeaf Publishing*

Web: www.bookleafpub.com

E-mail: info@bookleafpub.com

ISBN: 9789395755771

First edition 2022

*This anthology is dedicated to the
Ancestors, who paved the way for my voice
to be powerful enough to ring strong, clear
and true, and to the next Generations who
will be even louder than I.*

ACKNOWLEDGEMENT

I would like to thank all those powerful women who share their words, their hearts so beautifully. I want to thank the Aunties who are tough and soft in their love showing us how brave it is to be vulnerable. I have a long way to go, but have the best teachers and everything I learn and unlearn is in a good way.

PREFACE

...Or Something is an anthology I've been unknowingly writing for years, even when I wasn't writing. Those feels, those fears that have been trapped beneath the surface are ready to come out, even if I still can't say them out loud. I hope between these lines you find the courage to acknowledge your "or something", dig for it, love it, hold it, and cherish it - and then when you're ready, share that with your world.

Everything Is Okay - Debut

The sun shines down on me as I lay in the tall,
tickly grass,
I breathe in deeply, and everything is okay.

The sun gleams high above me in a bright blue
sky,
I breathe out slowly, and everything is okay.

I watch scattered fluffy clouds floating lazily
around the sky,
I breathe in deeply, and everything is okay.

The bright afternoon sun warms my skin
I breathe out slowly, and everything is okay.

The warmth from the sun touches my soul,
setting it ablaze,
As I breathe in the world around me and know
everything is okay.

As she lays in that tall tickly grass, she closes
her eyes to the bright yellow sun above her.
From behind closed lids she sees dancing lights,
sparkling yellows and quick reds flash, as the
sun puts on a show just for her.

The grassy field she lays in, is bright and green,
with flecks of purple around her from the tall
bunches of wild lavender that grew there. She
takes in a breath, deep through her nose,
inhaling the smell of the fresh air around her and
instantly a wave of calm washes over her. She
breathes out, a slow gust of hot air escaping her
lips.

I open my eyes and stand up from that place,
Getting ready to move forward with peace.

As I walk through life, I move with hope.
Knowing not every day will be perfect,
But a perfect moment can be found in each day.

There is beauty in the everyday;
The laughter of children
Hugs from loved ones
Whispers of a memory almost forgotten.

These little things bring a smile to my face
As I stand up, and leave this place.

Recently she learned the truth of her past, my
families past. The real truth, hidden in Canadian
Cruelty – should she trademark that? – was
overwhelming to accept at first. Residential
schools and stolen land, stolen names and

hidden children…she wanted to cower, cry,
scream at how wrong this world can be, the hurt
it can do to people.

Instead, I take in that deep breath,
And remind myself that everything will be okay.

I look for that beauty in the world
Actively I look, and uncover the beauty well
hidden.

Barefoot I walk through the tickly grass
Inhaling that sweet grass and lavender smell

I let my own inner child laugh
Dancing in circles under the hot yellow sun

My soul is nourished thinking of the power
Of my beautiful, strong and resistant ancestors.

That power lingers today,
In social movements grown bigger than the
individual
In acts of love celebrated in the face of hate
In times of teaching where there exists wilful
ignorance
The power is continuing to move forward with
hope.

Power also lies in;
Finding joy
Finding love
Finding peace

No – Power lies in;
Creating joy. Creating love. Creating peace.

Power knows the trauma of my past, my families
past,
Power chooses to move forward with hope.

Power is being positive,
When the world is filled with negativity.

Power is finding the perfect moment in each day,
Knowing that each day is inherently imperfect…

She finds herself seeking moments of quiet and
peace, in order to actually feel at peace. She
looks for the beautiful moments in life and
chooses to bask in them like she basks in the
sun. She listens for, and hears the laughter of
children and lets out her inner child to dance for
a moment. Giggling in whirling, twirling circles,
her inner child soars. She listens to loud music,
happy music, dancing music. She falls in love
and her soul burns along with the midday sun.
After twirling and whirling and giggling and

laughing and loving she falls back into that tall
tickly grass…

The sun shines down on me as I lay in the tall,
tickly grass,
I breathe in deeply, and everything is okay.

The sun gleams high above me in a bright blue
sky,
I breathe out slowly, and everything is okay.

I watch scattered fluffy clouds floating lazily
around the sky,
I breathe in deeply, and everything is okay.

The bright afternoon sun warms my skin
I breathe out slowly, and everything is okay.

The warmth from the sun touches my soul,
setting it ablaze,
As I breathe in the world around me and know
everything is okay.

When the World is Burning

When the world is burning,
Mother Earth continues to provide for us
Lovingly nourishing us, lifting us, catching us
when we fall;
Reminding us that she is our first mother, our
always and forever home.

When the world is burning,
Water, our life blood, continues to flow
Pooling, streaming, when angry - crashing;
Reminding us that nothing can remain the same.

When the world is burning,
Father sky continues to dazzle us with changing
colours
With help from Grandfather Sun and
Grandmother Moon;
Reminding us that with each sunset and sunrise,
change is constant.

When the world is burning,
Everything begins to change, you, me, us.
You remind me that nothing can remain the
same;
You become a new always and forever home.

When the world is burning,
Somehow, I missed these changes
They crept up, in that constant evolution;
Reminding me that while it burns, the world also
turns.

Everything is High

When I'm up, I can't come down.

I breathe out fast and hard,
Like I've been running.

Chased only by expectations,
Which, when I run fast enough,
Couldn't possibly keep up with me

The elation I feel is untouchable,
When I am up here,
I am untouchable.
And it feels great.

That power I find and create,
Is crackling at my fingertips,
All wild electric energy,

Unsure of where to use that energy,
I spark and burn,
Dangerous to others if they get too close.

My mood unmatched I soar,
High in the sky,
Living for a moment in bliss.

Everything is Low

When I'm down, I can't get up.

I breathe in, slow and shaky,
Like my lungs are as tired as I feel.

Dragged by all the expectations,
Unable to escape their clutch,
Knowing I couldn't possibly break free.

The despair I feel is inescapable,
When I am down here,
It is all encompassing.
And it is terrifying.

It leaves me feeling weak.
Unable to claim any kind of power,
Crackling energy dissipated;
I am dangerous to no one,
When I am trapped in my low mind

My mood unmatched I sink,
Low in the ground,
Surviving this moment in misery.

Contradictions

Always so kind and immensely sweet,
He easily sweeps her off her feet.

Her smile and eyes shine bright,
Her outlook for the first time light.

But she gets scared, it's all too fast,
And suddenly she's reminded of the past.

Fallen hard and wound up broken,
Her shattered heart leaves words unspoken.

He opens up, tells her how he feels,
She closes up, stepping back she reels.

He walks away, hurt and sad,
She stands alone, hurt and mad.

Mad that she fears being hurt once more,
Once he's gone she falls to the floor.

She sits in her room alone and cries,
Hating her fear she begs to know why.

He tells himself to move on and forget,

But what they could be is his biggest regret.

He forces himself to see someone new,
Deep down knowing its not true.

He moves away focusing on his dream,
She sees his happiness, comes apart at the seam.

He comes back home excited to see her,
She is nothing but nerves thinking of what they
were.

Not just of what they were but what they could
have become,
If only her heart hadn't been torn and undone.

She's torn about having him back, feeling the
heat,
Because every time he smiles her heart skips a
beat.

As happy as she is though she wishes he
wouldn't stay,
Because he's easier to love from far, far away.

Wrong For Me

Dark hair and burning eyes,
She's a product of heartbreak's demise.

Wounded eyes and a broken soul,
The dementia of their love took its toll.

Could they ever be fixed,
With feelings so badly mixed.

Hate and love, love and hate,
What a cruel thing, this debate.

Every touch so electric,
When did it become so hectic.

A love so destructive,
What a way to live.

Not an end in sight,
Break her heart he just might.

And what of his heart?
Does it hurt when they part?

Do his eyes burn and sting?

Hearing the phone ring and ring.

And yet despite all this,
It only takes one kiss.

To forget all the pain,
And fall in love again.

Waves

Have you ever cycled between the emotions,
Of joy and sadness in such a short amount of
time
That it takes your breath away
With the suddenness of a sharp inhale?

Stuck in the cycle of an inability to move on,
But a desire to forget the past.
The two emotions at war,
The cycle continuing.

Clashing

Clashing in the middle,
Forming a formidable wall of impenetrable
current;
Giant waves of emotion you are unable to
contain.

Waves

Waves crashing over your head,
You gasp for air,
But there is only

Desire

Desire threatening to overwhelm the senses.
Paralyzed with fear and an inability to act.
Scared of the ability to love,
But more of the ability to hurt and be hurt.

Relationships - Pretty Sure I'm Doing This Wrong

Angry
Her blood boils in rage,
The two, never on the same page.

Ashamed
She knew what he was,
What he always does.

Broken
Tears burning at her eyes,
Trying to navigate all the lies.

Hurt
Her heart is shattered,
She thought she mattered.

Stunned
How again did she fall?
How had she believed it all?

Silent
She ignores his pleas,
He begs on his knees.

Apologies
Her resolve disappears,
And down spill the tears.

Forgiveness
He pulls her in for a kiss,
A moment of bliss.

Promises
He promises to be there,
His head buried in her hair.

Worries
She wonders if he will stay,
Or whether or not he'll pull away.

Love
But regardless she'll wait,
Knowing he's her soul mate.

Rom Coms Lied

Romantic comedies, are full of lies,
Learning which, was a terrible surprise.

And maybe I shouldn't be learning from the
screen,
But the real world can be so mean.

But, they leave out the important stuff,
About what to do, when things get tough.

What they don't tell you, what they leave out,
Is that anxiety will leave you with crippling
self-doubt.

Self-esteem issues aren't aren't so quirky and
cute,
When they start to intrude on every romantic
pursuit.

A negative, broken, untrusting relationship with
your dad,
Is the opposite of sexy and hot, it just makes
things bad.

Breakdowns when things start to get real,

Because rom coms definitely don't teach you
how to heal.

And guess what, here's the worst part,
That guy you think is right? 100% going to
break your heart.

I'd like to see the rom com sequel,
Where relationships are built on footing that's
equal.

I want to see the real stuff, the mess, the fights,
The people staying up, crying through nights.

I want to see how people make-up, get through
it,
I want to know how to learn to commit.

I want to see people dealing with their fear,
Not just see it magically disappear.

I want radical truth and honesty in romance
depictions,
Not these ridiculously crafted absolute fictions.

The Sidewalk Ended

What they didn't tell me about the sidewalk
ending,
Is that it ended in a road that was dangerous.

And I don't mean dangerous as in
Cars moving too fast or
Beating the traffic light to cross the street;
I mean dangerous as in unknown.

Stepping out is hard when you don't know the
road.
When the terrain is not what you planned,
You have to step back, and reevaluate.

The Sidewalk Ended, and I needed to find my
place.
I was told about all the places I could end up,
But not how hard it might be to get there.

What they didn't tell me about the sidewalk
ending,
About that place where I would find my
imagination,
Is that it could be a dangerous place.

Thanks to Anxiety and Depression,
The monsters that lurk in shadows;
Preying on our deepest insecurities.

But, it was not just danger at the end of the
sidewalk.
It was also a place of bravery, creativity and
vibrancy;
Where we can find all the skills to battle
imagination monsters.

At the end of the sidewalk,
I found myself, the whole spectrum that makes
me, me.

Everything is Okay - Mezzo

The sun disappears as I lay in that tall, tickly
grass,
I breathe in deeply, and taste a storm coming in.
Everything does not feel okay.

The sun hides behind grey clouds, angrily
rumbling,
I breathe out as the first thunder rumbles in.
Everything does not feel okay.

I watch the lightning crackling in the distance,
I breathe in, a sigh realizing I should leave this
place.
Everything does not feel okay.

Before the storm rolls in and drenches me,
I breathe out, sometimes everything does not
feel okay.
Everything does not feel okay.

As she lays in that tall tickly grass, she closes
her eyes as the first drops hit her face. From
behind closed lids the dancing lights, sparkling
yellows and quick reds flash are over, the show
the sun was putting on is gone.

The grassy field she lays in is still that bright
green, with flecks of purple around her from the
tall bunches of wild lavender that grew there.
But today, the colours seem muted, dulled by the
impending storm. The same lavender that
usually brings calm, brings sadness as she
reminisces on times with her Nan, gone too long
now. She breathes in a shaky inhale, and out
comes a sob damp air rushing past her lips.

I open my eyes and stand up from that place,
Getting ready to move forward with unease.

As I walk, that hope is harder to find.
Today is the day that is not perfect,
And the perfect moment seems impossible to
find.

The beauty seems distant today;
The laughter of children,
Hugs from loved ones,
Whispers of a memory almost forgotten.

These little things make me tear up today,
As I stand up, and leave this place.

There are days where that knowledge of her
past, my families past, is all too much. It catches

up and steals your breath, whisking it away the
way the government whisked away children, her
ancestors, my ancestors. Some days, she does
cower, cry, scream at how wrong this world can
be, the hurt it can do to people.

I remind myself, to take that deep breath.
Not every day is like this; there is hope.
Even when everything does not feel okay.

I remind myself, find the beauty,
Insist that I look, and uncover beauty well
hidden.
Even when everything does not feel okay.

Stealing back stolen breaths,
I choose to dance as the rain comes.

Barefoot I twirl until the colours are bright
again,
Inhaling the sweet grass and lavender smell,
Until the sadness washes away,
And a watery smile spills over my face.

I remind myself of that found power;
I remind myself more of the created power;
Power knows the trauma of my past, my families
past,
Power chooses to move forward with hope.

She finds herself powering through the panic,
the sadness, the despair. Dancing in the rain
helps, water washing over her. Water washing
over her reminding her of Mother Earth's life
blood, the water that is cleansing her spirit,
healing the ancestors. Rain washing away the
dulled colours, leaving everything bright, shiny,
and loud once again, the thunder crashing as she
twirls through the field. She is not surviving or
weathering the storm, I am the storm.

Even when everything does not feel okay.
I breathe in, I breathe out,
And everything is okay.

Dark Days

When I think of a dark day,
I think of one congested with tasks,
Many people lined up with many asks.

I think of time indoors,
Back to back business, stagnant inside air
Eyes glued to a screen, often whispering
Do I really care?

Dark days mean extra loud voices.
An inability to quiet the external voices giving
tasks, jobs, responsibilities;
Or the internal voices, anxiety, pressure,
depression.

Dark days mean listening when I don't want to,
Pressure forcing the job done, despite the voices.
Anxiety, not enough time; Depression, why
bother?
The jobs always get done.

Dark days mean glancing out the window,
Longing to watch Mother Earth and Father Sky
dance;
Waiting for the next bright day,
When I can hear it, see it.

Bright Days

When I think of a bright day,
I think of a glowing sun warming my body,
With a gentle breeze whispering across my skin.

I think of time outdoors,
Spent in the woods or mountains,
With all of Mother Earth's beauty vast and
surrounding.
Reminding me of her unconditional love for me.

Bright days mean quieting the voices,
Both external voices crowing me with tasks, jobs,
responsibilities;
But also the internal voices, anxiety, pressure,
depression.

Bright days mean shutting off all those voices,
Instead listening to the stirring of trees,
Bubbling of springs,
Wind dancing as it blows by.

Mother Earth and Father Sky perform a dance of love
Father Sky sending the breeze to rustle Mother's
Earth's trees;
A bright day is quiet enough for me to hear it, see it.

Balancing Act

Life is a beautifully complicated balancing act.
It's full of downs and ups, and ups and downs.
Life can make you want to scream sometimes,
But just as often it can make you cheer;
Each end of the spectrum delightfully necessary.

I've always had a hard time negotiating balance.
I've had the highest of highs,
I've had the lowest of lows.
But navigating that in between space,
Proves the biggest challenge of all.

I don't know what it is about me,
That makes me go zero to one hundred.
I've always had an all or nothing mindset,
Challenging that has been hard,
But necessary as I navigate the balancing act.

I tend to leap before I look, that's true.
Overwhelming desire to see and do it all,
Neglecting the time and space to be quiet.
Both are necessary in the balancing act.

There can be Dark Days
And there can be Low Lows

While we love and cherish,
The Bright Days
And the High Highs.

So long as we don't forget the middle days.
Where magic can be created.
Where comfort rests.
Where we learn to unlearn.

In the middle days,
We dance in the great balancing act,
Learning the difference between;
Dark Days and Bright Days,
Highs and Lows,
Wrong For Me and Right For Me.

Understanding that,
Contradictions can be beautiful.
Waves are dangerous, but also magnificent,
And of course,
That Everything is Okay.

Maybe I Was Wrong

Maybe I was wrong about rom coms.
Maybe, they didn't fill my head with lies,
Maybe I was detonating the ticking bombs.
Maybe it was me, as I cherry picked the worst
guys,
And maybe missed something, in front of my
eyes.

For the longest time, I blamed only me.
Thinking every relationship was destined to
suck,
Solely because I constantly chose to flee.
But maybe it wasn't just rotten luck,
Maybe deep down I knew, my head and heart
were stuck.

I think I was picking relationships with too
much salt,
Not comfortable in my own skin, I made myself
small.
Blaming everyone, when no one was at fault
I backed myself against a wall.
Too scared in my immaturity, to be ready for it
all.

I was my own worst enemy in romance,
Basing relationships off of scripted fictions,
Playing it safe, secure, never taking the chance.
Rom coms and childhood trauma created too
many contradictions,
Loving you was too dangerous, I created
restrictions.

Maybe I was wrong about rom coms.
But here's the thing, they leave a lot of us out.
Admittedly yes, I was building relationship time
bombs,
But not once have I seen a "me" character
throughout,
So sorry rom coms, I guess I still have a little
doubt.

Right For Me

And for years I fell for the wrong boys;
All the while, cursing my inability to make
The right choices in relationships.
Often choosing those Wrong For Me.

But understanding that everything is about
perspective,
I've become a big believer lately,
That things happen when they're meant to
And that everything is a lesson
Guiding us towards our Right For Me.

I thought my Wrong For Me was the norm.
Not understanding that love isn't supposed to
sting,
That love should not be destructive in nature,
That love shouldn't always be dark and burning.

Love should be bright, warm but not burning,
Passion does not need to sting with it's
electricity,
It should be gentle tingles, sparks when you
touch;
Love does not come with broken promises and
constant tears,

Right For Me love shouldn't be contrite or
strained.

Right For Me love is easy like a breath of fresh
air,
Right For Me love picks me up when I fall,
It is never the one knocking me down.
Right For Me holds me with care,
Patient with all of my broken pieces.

I used to believe I was too broken for love,
That my fractured heart was too much
Too much for someone to hold so tenderly.
But my Right For Me constantly surprises me,
Gently reuniting the pieces until my heart is
whole,

Years of heartbreak had me convinced,
Convinced there was no Right For Me
That life would either be spent alone
Or with a lifetime of Wrong For Me

Then one day I opened my eyes
And saw for the first time
That Right For Me was there,
There the whole time.

Salted Love

When I was a child
My Nan used to put salt in my cuts;
She said it was to disinfect,
To clean,
That the sting was the salt working.

I used to cry to that sting
But her kisses reassured me;
It was okay, normal, healing.
There was nothing to worry about
Putting salt into that wound.

So I kind of liked that sting,
My child mind happy,
It's feeling the excitement.
The salt was working,
Cleaning my cuts, healing me

Loving you is putting salt in the wounds;
Wounds left open from years of bad decisions,
Bad boys who left me sad, broken.
Your love is the salt that cleans,
The salt that heals me

I sometimes cry with that sting

But your kisses reassure me,
It's okay, normal, healing.
You remind me that it's a journey

My adult mind happy,
It's feeling the excitement.
Your salted love is working,
The sting in the cuts
Is healing my heart

Bit by bit you give me salted love;
Reducing the amount of salt each time
So all that's left over
Is love.

Them

Heartbeats louder than a drum,
The feelings make her want to run.

Run fast and look the other way,
But just a mere smile makes her stay.

A smile that shines so bright,
Like a billion stars in the night.

Her laugh like music to his ears,
He sees the strength behind her tears.

He sees that her heart is bent but not broken,
Makes it his goal to fix with a promise left unspoken.

He makes her laugh and smile,
If only they could be alone for a while.

To say how they both feel,
The chemistry and connection so intensely real.

But the fear of what others might think,
Leave the two just on the brink.

Of something quite real and true,
With three little words: I love you.

Fireworks

This crazy thing that we have you and I,
It makes me want to both laugh and cry.
Never knowing what's in store
Both questioning what to explore.

The crying comes when I start to think,
Of all the barriers in our way;
The laughter when I let go and feel
Remember all the jokes and play.

We go together so well,
There doesn't need to be a kiss
To know without you I'd still be in hell;
One of my own creation, which I don't miss.

It shouldn't be this hard I know,
But to see that your smile stay on your face
Is what allows me to push forward and go.
Yours is a smile I choose to chase

Whoever said fireworks happen at a kiss,
Have clearly never known your smile,
Or the twinkle in your eye,
One that makes sparks fly.

So darling please hold on,
Because in not so long
It'll become so easy;
For me to love you and you to love me.

Togetherness

Togetherness is sitting curled up on the couch, a cup of hot tea warming your hand, under a cozy blanket while it rains.
It's that feeling of total comfort in a world that isn't always comforting.

Togetherness is sitting in the grass on a warm summer's day, the sun warming your skin, grass tickling your arms, watching clouds float by.
It's that feeling of total warmth in a world that isn't always warm.

Togetherness is sitting by a crackling fire, watching snow drift outside slowly, the air crisp and cool if you step out for a breath of fresh air.
It's that feeling of total peace in a world that isn't always peaceful.

Togetherness is laughing with friends, sitting and talking about nothing, while you talk about everything.
It's that feeling of trust, in a world that's not always trustworthy.

Togetherness is people smiling when you talk about your passions and interests, it's follow up questions that continue conversation.
It's that feeling of being heard, in a world that's not always listening.

Togetherness is the feeling of driving through mountains, watching them touch the sky, their trees growing despite the steep angles.
It's that feeling of wonder, in a world that's not always wonderful.

Togetherness is climbing into bed after a long day, glad to rest your body in a heap of pillows, blankets and sheets.
It's that feeling of safety, in a world that's not always safe.

Being with you is like all of these feelings rolled into one.
Togetherness with you is;
Comfort
Warmth
Peace
Trust
Heard
Wonder
Safe.

Everything is Okay - Finale

The sun moves in and out behind clouds;
The day might stay sunny,
The day might begin to storm,
Everything is complicated, but okay.

I breathe in deeply, everything is okay.
I breathe out slowly, everything is okay.

I watch stormy clouds swirling,
While enjoying the warmth of the sun.
Life is not black and white
It's a beautiful spectrum of colours in between.

I breathe in deeply, everything is okay.
I breathe out slowly, everything is okay.

As she lay there understanding the complexities of life, calmness begins to spread. This is the knowledge she has been missing as she moves through the big emotions, big feelings. These rolling hills and valleys of emotion are the most magical and human part of existence. Understanding that part of the balance of life is learning to ride the wave. She breathes in, she

breathes out knowing that despite it all,
everything is and will be okay.

Perfectly imperfect moments become
Imperfectly perfect memories.
Memories have a special way of touching our
souls,
A beautiful bridge between mind and heart.

I breathe in deeply, everything is okay.
I breathe out slowly, everything is okay.

Memories that once made me smile, make me
cry.
Memories that once made me cry, make me
smile.
Memories have a special way of touching our
souls,
A loving link between heart and mind.

I breathe in deeply, everything is okay.
I breathe out slowly, everything is okay.

The hardest teaching for her to learn from her
Elders was bravery, because she first learned it
from books and movies, a superhero type of
brave taking on villains. But bravery, true
bravery is moving with gentleness and
vulnerability in a world that tries to make us

hard. Taking off this hard shell, breaking down
the walls she had once built to protect herself,
was the biggest act of bravery she could
perform.

Power is not so linear, as I once thought.
Power is not either found or created,
Power is both simultaneously,
Power is navigated in the moment.

I breathe in deeply, everything is okay.
I breathe out slowly, everything is okay.

She still finds herself seeking moments of quiet
and peace, but she no longer needs it to feel at
peace. She knows now that she can always
create peace for herself. She lets out her inner
child to dance more often, she no longer needs
the prompts from giggling children, her inner
child's giggle is enough. Her inner child soars
because of how she takes care of her, always
encouraging giggling in whirling, twirling
circles now. She falls in love and her soul burns
along with the midday sun. She falls in love and
her soul is also the crashing storm when it needs
to be. And after all that twirling and whirling
and giggling and laughing and loving she falls
back into that tall tickly grass…

The sun gleams high above me in a bright blue
sky,
I breathe out slowly, and everything is okay.

I watch scattered fluffy clouds floating lazily
around the sky,
I breathe in deeply, and everything is okay.

The bright afternoon sun warms my skin
I breathe out slowly, and everything is okay.

The warmth from the sun touches my soul,
setting it ablaze,
As I breathe in the world around me and know
everything is okay.